MANAGING THE APPRAISAL

KT-504-098

FOLLOWING UP THE APPRAISAL

APPRAISING
STAFF

KEN LANGDON &
CHRISTINA OSBORNE

DK

Project Editor Nina Hathway
Senior Art Editor Jamie Hanson
DTP Designer Julian Dams
Production Controller Michelle Thomas

Managing Editor Adèle Hayward
Senior Managing Editor Stephanie Jackson
Senior Managing Art Editor Nigel Duffield

Produced for Dorling Kindersley by
COOLING BROWN
9–11 High Street, Hampton
Middlesex TW12 2SA

Creative Director Arthur Brown
Senior Editor Amanda Lebentz

First published in Great Britain in 2001
by Dorling Kindersley Limited,
9 Henrietta Street,
London WC2E 8PS

A CIP catalogue record for this book is available
from the British Library

ISBN 0 7513 2084 6

Reproduced by Colourscan, Singapore
Printed and bound in Hong Kong by Wing King Tong

See our complete catalogue at
www.dk.com

CONTENTS

INTRODUCTION

The ability to use appraisal to develop and motivate employees is a core management skill. Regular, constructive feedback on performance is vital if staff are to build on their strengths, achieve their full potential, and make the maximum contribution to their organization. Appraising Staff equips you with all the skills and techniques you need to conduct successful appraisals. It clearly explains the key aims and benefits of the appraisal process, and leads you step-by-step through the preparation, management, and follow-up of the appraisal interview. The book is packed with advice to help you encourage open discussion, interpret body language, build confidence, deal with performance problems, and more. With 101 practical tips scattered throughout and a self-assessment quiz that allows you to evaluate your skills as an appraiser, this is an invaluable pocket reference to appraising effectively.

UNDERSTANDING THE PURPOSE

Effective appraisal is at the heart of successful management. Understand how the appraisal process works, and recognize how a well-managed system benefits employees and organizations.

DEVELOPING PEOPLE

Regular feedback develops staff and helps them to achieve their objectives. Create an environment in which people welcome continuous feedback, and use the appraisal interview as a formal round-up of these on-going, informal reviews.

1 Encourage people to work to their full potential for successful results.

2 Praise good performance when you see it to motivate people to do even better.

PROVIDING FEEDBACK

All employees want to know how their performance is viewed by their manager. It is important to provide this feedback continuously, whether it is positive or negative. Proper feedback helps team members identify where they need to improve their skills, knowledge, and attitudes. Even highly successful achievers need feedback to help them sustain their performance. On-going feedback improves morale, since people know exactly where they stand, and enables managers to express concerns rather than storing them up.

APPRAISING FORMALLY

Formal appraisal interviews, held on a regular basis with your team members, are a culmination of continuous informal feedback. If on-going feedback has been effective, this formal meeting will not contain any surprises for appraisees, and the atmosphere should be positive and business-like. There are two parts to the formal appraisal: the performance review and the developmental review. The performance review enables you to gain agreement from an employee on how well he or she has done in achieving objectives, and developing skills and knowledge, during the period under review. The developmental review is aimed at pinpointing what needs to be done in future to sustain achievement or meet new objectives. This part of the appraisal helps you to continuously improve an appraisee's capabilities and prepare them to take on more responsibility. Do the two parts in one appraisal session to emphasize the link between them.

GETTING THE MOST FROM APPRAISAL

An effective appraisal system has many benefits. Use it to:
- Sustain motivation and commitment;
- Continuously improve performance;
- Give direction and agree expected contributions;
- Set targets in line with organizational and team goals;
- Review development so far;
- Identify training needs;
- Celebrate successes and learn from disappointments;
- Understand career aspirations and assess potential;
- Gather ideas for change.

| Provide continuous informal feedback | → | Formally review performance | → | Formally review development |

▲ DEFINING APPRAISAL

Effective appraisal relies on the provision of regular feedback. This feedback is then formalized in a two-part review of a team member's performance and development.

3 Make sure that people know how important they are to the organization.

APPRAISING EFFECTIVELY

Think carefully about how you will give feedback both formally and informally. In order to build for the future, it is important to be constructive in what you say and to focus on the future in the way that you say it. Make sure that all feedback is two-way, and that discussions are honest and open. Consider how you will put your points across, since people will react to the manner in which you provide feedback. Bear in mind that criticism can be difficult to take, even when an individual is aware that it is justified.

DEFINING APPRAISAL TYPES

There are three distinct types of appraisal, each involving a different approach to evaluating performance. Understand the purpose of top-down, peer, and 360-degree appraisals, and why self-assessment must feature in them all.

4 Ensure that staff understand how they will be appraised.

5 Find out how others in your organization view an appraisee's performance.

APPRAISING TOP-DOWN

Top-down appraisal means that the appraisee's immediate manager, who knows the appraisee best, is responsible for their appraisal and has the authority to agree a development plan for the future. Some companies use a "matrix" approach in which one manager appraises an individual in terms of their contribution to a specific office or region, while another manager appraises their input to their specfic area of work. A human resources specialist, for example, with an objective of putting employees on new contracts, would be assessed by a manager with human resources or legal expertise.

USING PEER APPRAISAL

In this type of appraisal, people at the same level appraise their peers, so that each appraiser can use his or her expert knowledge of the appraisee's role and responsibilities to give an authoritative opinion on their skills. Peer appraisal is often used in the professions, where specialist knowledge of issues such as ethics or technical competence is important. By monitoring colleagues as part of the appraisal process, changes in practice can be fed back to the profession, and improvements made to the way in which members behave and carry out their work.

POINTS TO REMEMBER

● Peer appraisal enables colleagues to act as mentors to one another, helping to improve performance all round.

● The exchange of open feedback among staff must be actively encouraged to ensure the effectiveness of peer appraisal.

● A combination of top-down and peer appraisal is often used to broaden the scope of feedback.

UNDERSTANDING 360-DEGREE APPRAISAL

In this type of appraisal, the appraiser seeks feedback from everyone who has worked with the appraisee, including customers, their peer group, and members of their own team. Generally, the appraiser will send out forms or questionnaires, such as customer satisfaction review forms, and then take comments into account when preparing for the formal interview. There is a growing trend towards this type of appraisal, since knowing how an appraisee's manager, peers, internal customers, external customers, and others view his or her performance often provides valuable insights.

6 See that questions on customer forms provide useful feedback.

7 Evaluate feedback carefully to ensure its value to the appraisee.

USING SELF-ASSESSMENT

Self-assessment encourages employees to play an active role in the appraisal process. The fact that people tend to be hard on themselves in a self-assessment can make the appraisal more successful. As their manager, you are likely to be less harsh, and can focus on positive aspects of their answers, praising achievements and strengths. Self-assessment questions should be framed to ensure that they help the appraisee to analyze their performance effectively. Answering the questions set should enable the appraisee to prepare for the appraisal itself, and to uncover any need for change. Avoid posing questions designed to lead an appraisee into giving evidence to support your own preconceived opinions. This will not result in a constructive appraisal.

ENCOURAGING ▶ REFLECTION

Self-assessment helps staff to feel included in the appraisal process. It prompts them to consider where they are going and how they are doing.

SETTING OBJECTIVES

Appraisals provide the opportunity to establish objectives in line with an organization's strategy. Bear in mind that up-to-date job descriptions are vital if you are to use appraisals to discuss, revise, and align objectives to your organization's aims.

8 Plan ahead and make allowances for any future changes.

9 Ensure that you are prepared for the arrival of new employees.

PRIMING NEW EMPLOYEES

The process of setting objectives will begin as soon as a new member of staff joins your team. Induction sessions should be used to introduce newcomers to the aims of your organization, and follow-up meetings should be held afterwards to ask new employees for feedback on the induction, agree job descriptions, and set performance objectives. If you fail to hold this meeting, a new recruit could be working for months before appraisals take place. Use the meeting to pinpoint training needs, identify other members of staff to be met, and plan future development needs.

DOCUMENTING OBJECTIVES

Every team member needs an up-to-date job description so that they understand what is expected of them and what their objectives are. The process of agreeing and documenting job descriptions can be done separately from the appraisal to enable team members to see where they need guidance or training to perform well. Be aware that roles may change between appraisals, since an individual's talents or interests in different aspects of their job can change its very nature. Appraisals enable you to update job descriptions and ensure that a team member's focus is in line with that of the team and the organization.

POINTS TO REMEMBER

● Setting aside a little time every couple of months to check through and update job descriptions makes it easier to spot any changes.

● Job descriptions should clearly define overall work objectives, broken down into key areas of activity.

● Job descriptions should be as succinct as possible – ideally fitting on to one A4 page – and should list main responsibilities rather than detail daily activities.

DEFINING THE PROCESS OF SETTING OBJECTIVES

Induction session is held to introduce new staff to organizational objectives

Follow-up meeting is held to define responsibilities and individual/team objectives

Job descriptions are agreed and documented to provide focus and direction

Job descriptions are reviewed regularly to maintain team and organizational focus

Appraisals are used to discuss and refocus individuals if their job emphasis has changed

Job descriptions are updated if necessary, and new objectives agreed

11 Try to turn good intentions into actions.

PLANNING FOR DEVELOPMENT

Just as there is a strong link between the objectives of teams in an organization, so there is a connected set of training plans. By reviewing training and development needs at each appraisal, you will be able to match an individual's requirements to those of their team and the organization. The appraisal and each development plan are important sources of information for organizations to plan training requirements. Personal development plans (PDPs) should specify the results you want to achieve, so that people develop in a way that helps them to achieve their objectives.

10 Use appraisals as an opportunity to ensure that people are realistic about their potential.

ESTABLISHING LONG-TERM GOALS

In addition to focusing on today's results, appraisals will help you to plan for the long term. By considering the potential of each team member, and discussing their career aspirations with them, you will be able to create a picture of your team in the future and produce a succession plan. Use the appraisal to identify when it is time for an individual to move on. Consider what you will do if someone is suddenly promoted off your team, or there is a change to your role. By planning ahead, you avoid the risk of failing to deliver results during a period of transition. You also ensure that other team members are not disrupted by change and are able to maintain consistent performance.

ACHIEVING OBJECTIVES

In addition to setting objectives for every employee, appraisals help to focus people on achieving them. By agreeing challenging, realistic, and quantifiable performance measures, you and your team members will be clear on how progress will be assessed.

12 See that measures of performance are challenging but achievable.

13 Set stretching but realistic targets that will motivate your staff.

14 Use objectives as a way of getting the team to focus and work together.

SETTING PERFORMANCE MEASURES

A key aspect of the appraisal is to communicate objectives with measurable criteria. Make sure that performance is measurable in numeric or percentage terms to provide appraisees with specific targets, and give them a sense of achievement when they surpass them. Encourage appraisees to come up with their own ideas as to what they should accept as a challenge. They will be more committed if they declare what is feasible themselves. Bear in mind that appraisees will often set themselves bigger challenges than those presented by an appraiser. People will rarely suggest a target that is well below what they believe they can achieve.

MAKING OBJECTIVES SMART

In a good appraisal environment, objectives are tested to ensure that they are specific, measurable, agreed, relevant, and timebound (SMART). Make your objectives SMART by ensuring that they:

● Clearly explain what the individual is meant to achieve – setting out exactly what must be done, how, and by when;

● Are measurable in terms of efficiency (resources used) and effectiveness (quality of result);

● Are proposed by the appraisee and agreed by appraiser after discussion;

● Are well within the appraisee's capabilities and control;

● Have a clear, unequivocal, and agreed timescale for completion.

SELECTING APPROPRIATE CRITERIA

Some performance measures cannot easily be translated into quantitative targets. Outcomes can be expressed in a number of ways, which means that it is important to select criteria that are appropriate to the individual and the particular objective. For example, in setting a performance measure for the writing of a report, an appropriate qualitative measure might be that the recipient would be able to make a confident decision after reading it. A qualitative objective, such as fast response to customer queries, may become a quantitative one if you decide to measure how many times the telephone rings before it is answered. An alternative qualitative measure could derive from a customer questionnaire that seeks feedback from customers as to whether they are satisfied with the standard of service they receive. In order to help you and the appraisee find the correct measure, ask yourselves the question, "What will success look like or feel like?"

QUESTIONS TO ASK YOURSELF

Q Do I understand what our customers expect from the appraisee?

Q When we agree a qualitative measure of performance, will we easily see later whether or not it has been met?

Q Is there any way we could turn a qualitative measure into a quantitative one?

Q Are we agreeing new measures that expect performance to improve in the future?

15 Be prepared to be flexible, if necessary, should a situation change.

AGREEING ▶ MEASURES

Although Sally had set the objective of improving the standard of her report writing, she was unable to raise her level of performance because Tom had failed to provide her with sufficient information By agreeing clear measure and expectations, he provide Sally with qualitative an quantitative measures to ai for, and her performan improved dramatically.

CASE STUDY

Tom, a marketing manager, was concerned that reports written by his assistant, Sally, were poorly structured and inaccurate. He often found himself correcting her drafts several times. During her appraisal, it was agreed that Sally should work to improve her report writing. However, after several weeks, Sally's work was still not up to the standard Tom required. He realized that in failing to set performance measures, he had not given Sally the guidance she needed to achieve her objective. He sat down with Sally and together they agreed that in future Sally's reports should follow a set template, starting with a 500–600 word introduction and ending with a summary of the main points. They also agreed that Sally would check all facts so that Tom need make no more revisions to her drafts. As a result, Sally began to produce highly professional reports.

EMPOWERING STAFF

Team members must be committed to objectives if they are to carry out their tasks successfully. Use appraisals to empower staff through delegation, to gain their commitment to actions, and to encourage them to use their own initiative.

 16 Work on the basis that everyone will want to do a good job.

DELEGATING CONTROL OF OBJECTIVES

Agree objective with team member

Allow team member to plan activities

Agree team member's plan

Ask team member to suggest options if plan needs to change

Agree performance measures with team member

17 Ask team members for their views on the way ahead.

EMPOWERING PEOPLE

By delegating responsibility to team members, you increase their control over what is achieved. This is because effective delegation involves the manager and team member agreeing on a specific and unambiguous statement of the objective and responsibility. The team member is then able to work on their own to achieve the objective, using their initiative to solve any problems along the way. Build an empowered environment by encouraging your team members to be less dependent on you as their manager. This will increase their effectiveness and save you time. Stress that you would prefer people to come to you with solutions rather than problems, particularly during the appraisal interview. Encourage them to analyze difficult situations, to consider ways of resolving them, and to recommend appropriate actions.

DOS AND DON'TS

✔ Do allow people to learn from their own mistakes.

✔ Do encourage people to think of different options for solving a problem.

✘ Don't assume you will always have the best answer to a situation.

✘ Don't allow people's mistakes to cause them to fail in a significant objective.

MAXIMIZING OWNERSHIP

CLARIFYING RESPONSIBILITIES ▼

During the appraisal, encourage the team member to take notes of what needs to be done. They will then be able to refer to their notes to help them summarize their action plan at the end of the meeting.

Once the achievement of an objective has been delegated, the appraisee must fully accept its value and be committed to seeing their action plan through to success. When agreeing objectives and plans at the appraisal, you must both be clear what the outcome of actions should be. Without commitment, you risk the appraisee delegating the task back to you, perhaps just before the deadline. If someone is reluctant to take on responsibility, you will need to find out why they have reservations. If an appraisee doubts their capabilities, consider how to alter the objective so that they feel able to achieve it, or organize training or guidance to build the person's competence and enable them to do the job confidently.

ENCOURAGING INITIATIVE

Use the appraisal to establish how you would like the appraisee to approach their work. You will not be getting involved in discussions on how they are going to go about achieving their objectives, but you should be concentrating on what needs to be achieved. You should let the appraisee know that you have faith in their ability and make it clear that you will be expecting them to use their own initiative. You will be setting agreed milestones to review progress so that you avoid continually asking for updates. Remember that it is important to give praise when staff make appreciable progress. "Thank you" and "Well done" are two of the most motivational phrases in the workplace.

POINTS TO REMEMBER

- People who feel able to achieve an objective in their own way will take more responsibility for that achievement.

- Good team leaders praise their people for finding new ways of getting results.

- The decision to do something is not complete until the first action is taken.

- People will take a more active part in the process of delegation if they are encouraged to question briefs and ask for more delegated responsibility.

REWARDING SUCCESS

Effective appraisal enables you to reward achievement and encourage continuous improvement. Plan to use appraisals to discuss rewards that satisfy the needs of the individual and the organization, rather than focusing on pay reviews alone.

18 Make sure that rewards are in keeping with your organization's goals.

19 Always deliver rewards that have been earned by team members.

PRESENTING PRIZES ▼

Awarding prizes or holidays is a good way of celebrating and recognizing achievement. Find out from team members during their appraisals how they would like to be rewarded for good performance to give you more ideas for non-financial rewards.

BREAKING THE PAY LINK

There is a link between what an employee is paid and their value to the organization. You may need to make judgments about the effect of a person's performance on the pay rewards they receive. To encourage excellent performance, find other ways to reward high achievers. These people are motivated by feedback and may well become de-motivated if they see low achievers receiving the same rewards. However, if the appraisal is seen as a hurdle that must be jumped in order to win a pay increase, an appraisee is likely to become defensive. For this reason, appraisals are often timed separately from pay reviews.

Team member receives prize as a reward for meeting objectives

Colleagues feel motivated to follow good example

This simplified model of pyschologist Abraham Maslow's hierarchy of needs illustrates the importance of satisfying needs at the lower levels before motivating people at higher levels. A car, a social need, may be motivational, but it will not be so until physiological needs have been met.

Self-actualization needs
(development of own potential,
finding self-fulfilment)

Self-esteem needs (approval
from others, recognition,
achievement)

Social needs (acceptance
from others, affiliation,
belonging)

Safety needs (feeling
of security, not
fearing danger)

Physiological needs (basic
requirements of life, such as
food and drink)

Motivating People

Appraisals give you an opportunity to reward your team by thanking and motivating them. The fact that you are spending time alone with them and discussing their work is in itself encouraging. People like to know that their work is being observed by their manager. Most are also motivated by a sense of autonomy, where they feel responsible for achieving a result rather than just carrying out tasks. This helps them to feel more in control of their jobs. To keep your team motivated, delegate wherever possible. If a team member achieves success in a delegated task, their sense of achievement is a great morale-booster. Finally, think about what will motivate each individual, since everyone has different needs.

Building on Success

Use appraisals to develop your team by discussing past successes and achievements so that they can be repeated and even surpassed. Consider building on achievements by promoting a team member, or giving someone the chance to take part in development activities. In addition to rewarding the appraisee, this will also enhance their value to your organization and their ability to meet objectives. Review the period since the last appraisal and discuss how the appraisee has used the activities in their previous development plan to improve their capabilities. This discussion helps the individual to understand the value of the development activities they have undertaken and shows them how they are improving their ability to contribute to the team and organization.

20 Find out what it is that motivates each member of your staff.

21 Remember that success often breeds further success.

PREPARING TO APPRAISE

Good preparation is an essential part of appraising effectively.
Plan every aspect of the discussion thoroughly and ensure that
appraisees are well prepared to ensure a successful outcome.

BEING PREPARED

The appraiser and appraisee have specific responsibilities in an appraisal. To ensure that the discussion is focused and controlled, understand your own role and brief appraisees on their responsibilities so that they, too, can prepare effectively.

 22 Make the most of your appraisal time by thinking about it in advance.

 23 Plan to talk about the job – not about the person.

24 Always check that you have all the documentation you need for appraisals.

DEFINING THE APPRAISER'S ROLE

The role of the appraiser is to encourage and guide the appraisee through the structure of the appraisal. You should be a conduit, or a catalyst, not a judge or interrogator. Plan the logistics of the meeting at least two weeks in advance. Note down the topics you wish to discuss in order of importance, so that you know in advance what you need to cover. Think of questions that will encourage the appraisee to talk. Read any guidance notes that accompany the appraisal documentation issued by your organization.

- An appraisee should be aware that he or she may need to make notes during the appraisal.

- Formal appraisals are more effective when the appraisee knows what to expect.

- A formal appraisal is very important to the appraisee, and the appraiser must prepare to meet those high expectations.

▼ HELPING APPRAISEES TO PREPARE

Self-assessment questions should be carefully framed to help appraisees prepare for discussion. Ensure that staff have ample space to be able to answer the questions as fully as possible.

UNDERSTANDING THE APPRAISEE'S ROLE

For the appraisee, the appraisal meeting offers an opportunity to discuss jointly their performance, their progress, their future, their objectives and focus, and their approach to the job. To help them prepare for this discussion, issue appraisees with a self-assessment document and give them plenty of time to complete it. Ask them to come up with examples of high and low points, and to think about areas for improvement. Have there been any changes to their job, or aspects that have become more or less important since the last review? Encourage people to report back on projects they have worked on, or suggest worthwhile projects for the future.

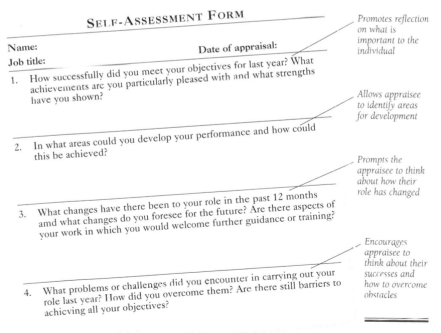

SELF-ASSESSMENT FORM

Name:

Job title:

Date of appraisal:

Promotes reflection on what is important to the individual

1. How successfully did you meet your objectives for last year? What achievements are you particularly pleased with and what strengths have you shown?

Allows appraisee to identify areas for development

2. In what areas could you develop your performance and how could this be achieved?

Prompts the appraisee to think about how their role has changed

3. What changes have there been to your role in the past 12 months amd what changes do you foresee for the future? Are there aspects of your work in which you would welcome further guidance or training?

Encourages appraisee to think about their successes and how to overcome obstacles

4. What problems or challenges did you encounter in carrying out your role last year? How did you overcome them? Are there still barriers to achieving all your objectives?

EVALUATING PERFORMANCE

Preparing for appraisal involves looking at an overview. Evaluate an appraisee's progress since the last review – in terms of performance and development – to help you set new objectives and plan activities effectively for the period ahead.

25 Align the job description with the organization, not the person.

26 Look for the causes of under-performance.

27 Review the facts and disregard rumour or hearsay.

REVIEWING JOB DESCRIPTIONS

Examine the appraisee's job description to ascertain whether roles or responsibilities have changed since the last appraisal. Ensure that any alterations are in the interests of the organization, and not just the appraisee. If, for example, a team member dislikes cold calling on the telephone, they may have moved the emphasis of the job towards serving existing customers instead of finding new ones. Rather than allowing the change to the job description, consider training the appraisee in telephone or tele-marketing techniques.

EVALUATING PROGRESS

Review the achievements of the appraisee against their specific objectives. Pick out good aspects of performance so that you can praise them, and encourage the appraisee to keep up their high standards. Have they approached their work positively? Have they planned, co-ordinated, and organized successfully? Where performance falls short of what is expected, consider the possible reasons. Ask yourself whether the area of under-performance is truly important. Negative feedback may not be necessary if an issue is minor, particularly when excellent results have been achieved in other areas.

THINGS TO DO

1. Check that the action plan agreed at the last appraisal was carried out.

2. If actions have not been completed, find out why.

3. Ascertain whether the appraisee has been rewarded and/or praised for carrying out tasks successfully.

28 Check whether staff have had the time to focus on development.

Appraiser finds out how team member has benefited from training in new software program

REVIEWING DEVELOPMENT

Having gathered information on an appraisee's job performance, review the benefits and effectiveness of their development activities. This is important not only to ensure continuous development, but also to confirm that the investment of time and money in developing the appraisee has been worthwhile. Ascertain whether the development objectives set at the last appraisal achieved what was expected. Check that the activities improved performance to a level that affected business results. Finally, review the performance of coaches and training organizations involved to ascertain how successful they were.

◀ CHECKING FOR QUALITY

Follow up on courses by seeking feedback from staff on their effectiveness. Invite them to demonstrate what they have learned and consider whether the team might benefit from a similar presentation.

IDENTIFYING PROBLEMS

When planned development activities have not been carried out, investigate why. Perhaps an appraisee was unable to attend a course because there was a crisis in the office. If so, find out whether losing the cancellation fee and wasting the trainer's time was truly warranted. Consider whether the appraisee still needs to carry out the activity. Could the need be met differently in the future? Assess whether the development activities were appropriate for the individual. For example, if after watching a video or reading a book, the information received was not applied, the appraisee may benefit from a different method of learning.

QUESTIONS TO ASK YOURSELF

Q Is the reason for any problem the appraisee may be having outside the appraiser's control?

Q What barriers restricted performance?

Q Were the objectives sufficiently clear?

Q Does the under-performance expose a development need?

Q Is the person capable of developing enough to perform to standard?

21

IDENTIFYING GOALS

Having evaluated performance, the next stage of preparation is to pinpoint areas for improvement and set objectives to achieve strategic business goals. Identify current levels of performance, and look for ways of developing skills and knowledge.

29 Bring objectives in line with the goals and policy of the organization.

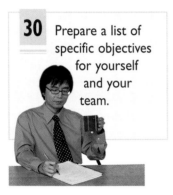
30 Prepare a list of specific objectives for yourself and your team.

FOCUSING ON TARGETS

Challenging yet achievable targets are essential if people are to feel motivated to improve performance and sustain high standards. Prepare for effective objective-setting with the appraisee by considering key result areas for their job. List these areas in order of importance, focus on up to six areas at the top of your list, and draw up suitable objectives for each. Phrase objectives carefully, using specific, active language, such as "sell" and "produce". Avoid vague or ambiguous terms such as "liaise" or "improve".

PREPARING MEASURABLE OBJECTIVES

Assign measures to each objective, ensuring that you will be able to access the information you need to monitor performance against those measures. Look, too, at team and organizational objectives and how these are measured. Consider the contribution that each team member must make towards this. For example, if the team's revenue target amounts to £2,000,000 and there are ten team members, you may wish to set everyone an objective of achieving £210,000. This divides the task evenly and ensures that if one person misses the target but everyone else achieves it, there is a good chance that the team will achieve its aim.

31 Be ambitious and always aim high when setting objectives.

32 Always try to be consistent in your expectations of other people.

SETTING STANDARDS

It is important to set standards, covering both the job and personal behaviour, by which competency can be measured. To help you do this, imagine what ideal performance would look like. In a customer service environment, for example, you may wish to see that staff have developed an efficient process for following up with customers as promised. Next, think how a high performer would typically behave – perhaps he or she would have the ability to listen actively and empathetically. Avoid focusing on the people who are currently doing the job and concentrate on the job itself and the desired results. Assess whether the appraisee is meeting the standards so that you can discuss development or praise progress in the appraisal.

33 Focus on what would be ideal, not on what is being achieved now.

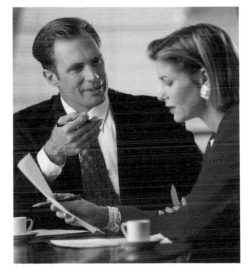

GAINING AN INSIGHT ▶
Find out more about the levels of competency needed to do a job successfully by talking to people with experience in the role. Speak to staff who have done the same work effectively or refer to outside experts in the field.

ASSESSING DEVELOPMENT NEEDS

Consider whether the requirements of a team member's role are changing and plan to prepare people for impending change before it occurs. If altering roles means that additional skills are required, assess whether the team member has already demonstrated those skills sufficiently, or whether there are any areas where they are lacking skills. If you identify a need for development, plan which activities would be appropriate. Prior to the appraisal, check that resources, such as a budget for training, will be available for the planned activities. Ensure, too, that you will be able to release the team member from normal duties during the training period.

PLANNING AHEAD

Effective planning for an appraisal involves anticipating an appraisee's needs and considering how best to respond to them. Be clear on what you are able to agree, and consider timing, resources, and allocating responsibility for agreed actions.

34 Have a good grasp of company policy on career development.

QUESTIONS TO ASK YOURSELF

Q Will I be able to make decisions on pay, time off or other rewards?

Q Am I in a position to promise that someone will be promoted or trained for further career progression?

Q Am I able to agree training and development and the budget necessary for it?

Q Do I have the authority to organize job transfers, secondments, or work experience on different projects or sites?

Q Will the human resources department agree that I have selected the best method of developing the individual?

DEFINING AUTHORITY

Make sure that you know what you will be able to agree on your own authority, and what needs authorization. If you are unsure about this when you come to conduct the appraisal, you risk reducing your credibility as a manager by raising an appraisee's expectations and then dashing them later. You may also lose the appraisee's trust if you are forced to renege on a promise that cannot be resourced.

Manager re-reads her organization's appraisal policy to check that she has not missed anything

BEING THOROUGH ▶
Familiarize yourself with company policies on matters such as holiday and expense allowances so that you will be in a position to answer questions on these issues. Be clear, too, on your organization's and team's aims to ensure that any objectives agreed will be in alignment.

35 Promise only things you can genuinely deliver.

36 Identify problems that may prevent an appraisee from achieving objectives.

PLANNING TIME AND RESOURCES

Estimate the duration, and start and finishing times, of the tasks necessary to achieve the objectives you have prepared for the appraisee. This will help you to ensure that what the appraisee suggests is realistically attainable. Estimate how much time is needed for development activities and assess whether you will need cover while the appraisee is away. Plan the resources needed both to achieve objectives and undertake development activities. Consider equipment, materials, and facilities such as working space. This well-prepared "project" plan will provide a starting point for your appraisal discussion.

ALLOCATING TASKS

Consider in advance who will be responsible for carrying out proposed actions after the meeting. For example, who will monitor any milestones agreed on the way to the objectives? Consider how exceptions or shortfalls could be reported. This task may be taken on by the appraisee, or you might take responsibility yourself, or ask a third party. After the appraisal, who should be responsible for researching and organizing development work, such as training? Finally, bear in mind that if the appraisee is to take ownership of the objectives, achieving them must be within their direct control.

37 Check that people have the time to lend their support.

Manager asks senior team member to act as a mentor to appraisee

ORGANIZING SUPPORT ▶
If there are members of staff who may be able to assist the appraisee in achieving their performance or development objectives, approach them before the appraisal to enlist their support. During the appraisal you can then let the appraisee know what level of assistance they can expect.

CREATING A POSITIVE ENVIRONMENT

A conducive appraisal environment encourages openness, receptiveness, and discussion. Build your credibility, create an atmosphere of trust, and pay attention to the layout of the meeting room to help the appraisee relax and feel comfortable.

38 Show respect for issues discussed in confidence with the appraisee.

39 Avoid telling an individual one thing and saying something else to another.

MAINTAINING CONFIDENTIALITY

To create an atmosphere in which both appraiser and appraisee can talk freely, it is important to stress that complete confidentiality is expected on both sides. Prior to the appraisal interview, make sure that you let the appraisee know which aspects of the discussion will be kept between the two parties, and what needs to be passed on to others, for example the Human Resources department. Having agreed to keep certain matters confidential, keep to your word and do not discuss them with anyone else.

BUILDING TRUST

Trust grows over time, and the stronger the relationship between appraiser and appraisee, the more effective appraisals will become. Earn your team's trust by putting into action decisions made during the appraisal. The reputation of an appraisal system can be ruined if what is said in the appraisal room turns out to be a series of good intentions that are never followed through. You will need to be assertive as a manager, but you should always be seen as honest, consistent, and fair.

POINTS TO REMEMBER

● Trust can take a long time to build, yet it can be destroyed within seconds.

● If an appraisee suspects that confidentiality might be broken, significant items may be held back.

● Taking a few moments before the appraisal to imagine yourself in your appraisee's shoes will help you to be on their wavelength.

SETTING UP THE ROOM

Create a relaxed ambience by choosing a suitable room and arranging office furniture so that there are no barriers between yourself and the appraisee. Make sure that the room is private so that you are not overheard, and that it does not have glass doors or panels – you do not want to be distracted by people walking past and looking into the room. Careful preparation of the meeting room shows the appraisee that you are genuinely interested in their achievements and development. Conversely, an unprofessional atmosphere will make the appraisee feel isolated and unimportant. Check that lights will not be shining in the appraisee's eyes or silhouetting you against the window so that they cannot see and read your expressions.

40 Plan to start the appraisal as you mean to continue – in a positive tone.

▼ ARRANGING THE DETAILS

When planning seating arrangements, aim to create the most informal, comfortable atmosphere possible. Using the corner of a desk is friendly, informal, and practical. It is easy to maintain good eye contact and is far less confrontational than sitting opposite one another.

Work at the same level by sitting on chairs that are of a similar size

Clear the work surface so that paperwork does not form a barrier between you

BEING OBJECTIVE

A manager's personal approach to an appraisal meeting is critical to its success. Prepare yourself for the discussion by considering how you will encourage ideas, avoid bias, and focus on the important aspects of the job.

 41 Ensure that you hold an objective appraisal – not a subjective review.

ENCOURAGING IDEAS

Remember that you are aiming to encourage people to come up with their own ideas and opinions. You will learn little about your team members, or their ideas, by simply telling them what to do. Frame questions that will prompt appraisees to voice their ideas and take ownership of what is agreed. For example, you could ask what difficulties they have faced and how they might overcome them next time. Your staff are likely to be far more knowledgeable about their jobs than you are. You also want to hear their opinions, not simply a reflection of your views.

AVOIDING BIAS

One of the key attributes of a good appraiser is the ability to stand back and think about an issue before making a decision. This is especially important when conducting appraisals, since it is vital to avoid jumping to conclusions based on superficial information. Many people tend to form opinions of others based on their past experiences of them, or may assume that an individual who shares one attribute with another person also has other qualities in common with them. There are a number of well-known types of bias that a good appraiser should learn to recognize to ensure that they are in the best position to avoid them.

RECOGNIZING TYPES OF BIAS

TYPE OF BIAS	RECOGNIZING THE SIGNS
HALO/HORNS	A tendency to allow one or two favourable or unfavourable personal attributes to colour your judgment, such as assuming that an attractive and articulate individual is also intelligent.
PREJUDICE	The judgment of an appraisee is clouded by personal views of a particular group or type of people, or the fact that they resemble or remind you of an acquaintance.
"SIMILAR TO ME"	A tendency to like people we see as being similar to ourselves and therefore to recruit, and even promote, in our own likeness. This leads to unbalanced teams, where all members have the same strengths.
DISTORTED PERSONALITY THEORY	The inclination to base an evaluation of appraisees on distorted personality traits, such as assuming that someone needs to be extrovert in order to be a good sales person.
GOOD WORKER	The propensity to have a mental image of a good worker, and to favour only those appraisees who match that image. This can result in unfair criticism of appraisees who fail to fit the stereotype.

42 Aim to ask an appraisee to express what success would look or feel like to them.

BEING RESULTS-ORIENTED

Make sure that the appraisal will be focused on what is important. If you discuss side issues at length, you risk misdirecting a team member's productivity by leading them to think that these are important. You should also avoid subjective or judgmental comments. Having set targets and standards for what is important, allow appraisees to express results in a way that makes sense to them. An appraisee's success criteria can be just as valid and motivating for them as quantitative criteria. Nevertheless, it is vital for you both to agree on what is to be measured, so that there are clear indicators of what has been achieved

PLANNING THE STRUCTURE

A good appraisal is well structured. Establish the order of proceedings, and plan to get the meeting off to a positive start. Then consider how to focus the appraisee on key areas for discussion and deliver feedback effectively.

43 Make sure that every appraisal follows the same six-step structure.

STARTING POSITIVELY

Always aim to begin every appraisal with a strong motivational statement and an easy question to ease the appraisee into the session and help them to relax. Next, you should agree on the purpose of the meeting, and outline what will be covered. Plan to say that you will review progress on each objective, one at a time. Aim to give the appraisee the chance to comment first, with questions such as, "How do you think your performance went in this area?" You will have the facts in front of you, both in terms of what has been achieved and of the feedback you are expecting to give. However, by allowing the appraisee to speak first, you encourage the process of self-assessment, and in identifying where you have different perceptions, you can explore the reasons why.

FOLLOWING THE SIX-STEP APPRAISAL STRUCTURE

Introduction — Establish the positive purpose of the meeting

Agenda — Agree items for discussion with the appraisee

Discussion — Initiate two-way communication

Action plan — Agree actions needed to achieve objectives

Summary — Ask appraisee to summarize agreed actions

Follow up — Monitor action plan and objectives

SETTING THE AGENDA

There is a limit to the number of issues you can effectively tackle during the appraisal, so plan to focus the appraisee on key areas so that you can agree a measurable number of objectives, say six. You may have other items to review, such as special projects, and the appraisee is likely to have their own items for discussion. It is important to remember that the appraisal is not the time to catch up on operational matters. You will be holding the discussion not as part of your day-to-day management of the team, but to review the individual's overall performance and skills, set new objectives for the period ahead, and agree a development plan. Any other business, such as a disciplinary matter, is outside the scope of the meeting and should be left out

44 Try to cut your planned agenda in half to see if that improves the focus.

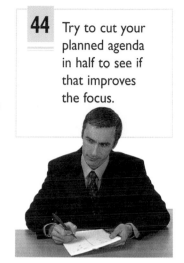

45 Focus on matters that have a direct impact on performance.

BEING CONSTRUCTIVE

If you have to give negative feedback, do so constructively, encouraging people to look forward, not backward. Avoid demotivating a potentially good appraisee by sounding over-critical. If performance has suffered, look first at your own leadership. Have you misjudged their level of skill, or failed to provide support? If there are no external reasons, then the appraisee needs to understand the impact of the problem. Plan how to tackle the issues constructively. How will you get them to acknowledge that a problem exists? Think of questions that will prompt the appraisee to find solutions. He or she will be more committed to resolving matters if the idea is their own.

MAINTAINING A POSITIVE TONE ▼
Aim to "sandwich" critical remarks between positive points of praise so that you keep the ratio of two expressions of praise to one expression of criticism.

Praise ➤ **Criticize** ➤ **Praise**

MANAGING THE APPRAISAL

Managing the appraisal involves careful choreography of the discussion. Become an effective appraiser by following a set format while remaining flexible at all times.

INTRODUCING THE SESSION

The start of a meeting sets the tone for what is to come. Launch the interview successfully by putting the appraisee at ease. Build their confidence, agree what will be discussed, and explain how the meeting will be conducted to give them time to relax.

 46 Make sure that the appraisee knows exactly what to expect.

 47 Put the appraisee at ease as quickly as possible.

48 Stress that the appraisal will have a positive result.

BUILDING CONFIDENCE

Many appraisees feel nervous and apprehensive at the start of their appraisal. Help them to overcome their anxieties by creating a welcoming, encouraging atmosphere. Address any uncertainties by stressing the positive purpose of the meeting and informing them how long you expect it to last. To build trust and confidence, begin with a motivational statement that conveys faith in their ability. Then ask an easy question to start them talking. Do not launch abruptly into the session by asking a challenging question early on, since this will cause the appraisee to feel defensive.

49 Check that you both set off in the same direction.

USING AN APPRAISAL DOCUMENT ▼

Ask the appraisee to fill in an appraisal document as you progress through the appraisal. This will save the time and effort of transcribing notes later. If it has been decided that you should fill in the form, show the appraisee what you have written and gain their assent on every category.

AGREEING THE PURPOSE

Establish the purpose of the appraisal interview to clarify why you are both there. Set out what you need to achieve from the appraisal, focusing on the advantages to the appraisee, so that staff truly believe that the appraisal will ultimately benefit them. Explain that you will be agreeing an agenda first, reviewing the previous period, discussing progress on objectives and how development needs were met, and pinpointing any further needs that have arisen. Establish that you will be agreeing objectives for the period ahead and then identifying any development needs linked to new objectives or responsibilities.

Purpose of job should be clearly defined in a brief summary

APPRAISAL DOCUMENT

Overall purpose of job:
To plan and design engineering projects to meet client specification within budget/time estimates.

Key areas of responsibility	Objectives	Deadline	Review comments on outcome
1. To manage the X Port development project.	1. To keep in touch with clients at agreed frequency and chair steering meetings.	Jan – Feb	
	2. To submit proposal by Feb 12 and obtain project by end of March.	March 31	
	3. To source project support to within 90% of requirements.		
2. To develop communications within design team.	1. To hold monthly meetings to review projects and communicate results within one week.	Review in April	
	2. Evaluate clarity of drawings and communicate results to staff twice a week or as required.	By June	

Responsibilities will be broadly summarized

Objectives should be described in a brief but specific statement

Dates for progress review meeting need to be recorded

AGREEING THE AGENDA

For an appraisal to run smoothly, both parties must agree on the items to be discussed. Alter your agenda to include some of the appraisee's ideas, explain how you will agree future objectives, and check that you have included all the important issues.

50 Focus on issues that are relevant to the objectives of the entire team.

51 Avoid being sidetracked by excessive or minor detail.

SEEKING INPUT

To ensure that the appraisee feels involved in the discussion you are about to have, ask them to add their own points to the agenda. Compare the importance of your agenda items with the topics that they wish to cover, and be prepared to change your agenda to accommodate them. Even if you regard their issues as less important, you must tackle some of them. If you ignore their concerns, they will feel that you are uninterested in their problems. By agreeing to include their points at this stage, you will also avoid problems later. An appraisee who has an axe to grind is likely to continue to attempt to bring the subject up, distracting you from your agenda. Be fair. If they are right, change the agenda.

Appraiser indicates agreed timing and suggests deferring some less important agenda items

◀ DISCUSSING TIME CONSTRAINTS

It is unlikely that there will be time to discuss all the items tabled. Make sure that you agree at the outset which items will be included on the agenda, and which points will not be covered, so that you can arrange a meeting to handle outstanding matters at a later date.

DEVELOPING OBJECTIVES

The aim of the appraisal is to develop a set of objectives that the employee is committed to achieving. Agree with the appraisee that you will discuss each previous objective in turn to identify what went well, what did not go so well, and what the appraisee can do about it. This may simply be to continue to maintain high standards, or to develop their skills in order to improve their performance. Establish that you will be setting future objectives in the form of a jointly agreed action plan, with criteria to measure success. You will also agree on the importance of objectives to the team, to the organization and, most importantly, to the appraisee if they are successful.

52 See that the appraisee participates fully in creating the agenda so that they feel included and involved.

ASSESSING THE AGENDA

Check that the agenda focuses on the appraisee's performance as it stands now. Do not assume, for example, that he or she will see the link between success in a past project and using the same skills on a new and different future project. Do not duck issues – you risk setting objectives that the appraisee will accept with no hope of achieving. Ensure that the agenda includes finding out what the appraisee believes is achievable. They may feel they can achieve more than you thought possible. You will discuss this and identify why your views differ. You may find that you think more is achievable than they do, and will need to plan support and confidence-building activities.

ORDERING ITEMS FOR DISCUSSION

Review previous objectives

Praise achievements

Give constructive feedback

Identify development needs

Praise additional achievements

Agree new objectives

Agree further development needs

Plan and agree actions

Summarize

ENCOURAGING DISCUSSION

In a successful appraisal interview, the appraisee should be doing most of the talking. Encourage staff to take a leading role in the discussion by adopting good questioning techniques, then listening actively to the answers.

53 Keep asking questions to gain the appraisee's involvement.

54 Avoid interrupting once an appraisee has started talking.

55 Consider how to turn most of your closed questions into open ones.

ASKING QUESTIONS

Good questioning techniques are essential if you are to discover an appraisee's true opinions. When you understand how an individual feels, you can use this knowledge to help them improve their performance. By asking the right questions you encourage an appraisee to bring issues into the open, rather than harbour a problem so that it festers and hinders performance. Use questioning in a genuine attempt to find out how the appraisee feels about all aspects of their job. Listen to their answers. Avoid cross-examining the appraisee or asking leading questions in a bid to confirm a pre-conceived notion in your own mind.

USING OPEN QUESTIONS

An open question encourages an expansive answer, as opposed to a closed question, which typically prompts a one-word "yes" or "no" response. Frame open questions by starting with the words, "What", "When", "How", "Which", "Who" or "Why". If you ask open questions, such as, "What were the main learning points?", an appraisee is far more likely to express their ideas than if you ask a closed question, such as "Did you achieve this objective?" Look at the objectives you will be reviewing and come up with an open question to start the discussion on each one.

56 If an appraisee looks confused, ensure you are not using jargon that they do not understand.

▲ LISTENING PROPERLY
Ideally, you should aim to spend about 80 per cent of the appraisal time listening, and only 20 per cent of the time speaking.

▼ SHOWING INTEREST
The appraiser in this example is an active listener; his body language demonstrates that he is giving his undivided attention to the appraisee and is concentrating on what is being said.

LISTENING ACTIVELY

Once you have encouraged the appraisee to start talking, listen actively to their answers. If you are listening actively, you will be able to glean far more from what is being said. Look at the appraisee and maintain good eye contact – but try to avoid staring. Bear in mind that even if you glance over their shoulder or out of the window, you will give the impression that you are not paying proper attention to what is being said. When the appraisee pauses, or draws to a conclusion, help them to build on their ideas by asking further questions. Be aware of the tone of voice that they are using, and listen out for subtleties of speech that may provide clues on what they truly think about their performance. This will enable you to build joint solutions by asking more questions such as, "What will help you to achieve even better results?"

Good eye contact is maintained

Appraisee feels encouraged to talk freely

Appraiser leans forwards to indicate interest

BEING PRACTICAL

There may be a long list of issues to discuss in an appraisal, most of them with significant implications for the future. Ensure that you keep to the agreed timing, tackle all the important items, and prompt appraisees to reach realistic conclusions.

 57 Aim to stick to the time allowed for the appraisal meeting.

 58 If an appraisee hints at any problem, address it immediately.

KEEPING TO THE POINT

Stick to the agenda and focus on essential issues by controlling the discussion so that it does not stray from the appraisee's previous important objectives or those for the future. It is important to complete the appraisal in the time allocated or you risk spending longer than you can afford on appraising the entire team, and may be forced to postpone some appraisals. If a discussion on one point has overrun, consider which agenda items you can shorten, miss out, or deal with at a later date.

COVERING VITAL ISSUES

If, as a result of time constraints, you are unable to discuss an important issue in sufficient depth, agree to have another conversation on the topic at a later date – and keep to that next date. Avoid using this as an excuse to postpone difficult issues; the sooner these are out in the open, the better. If there is a hint that an appraisee is experiencing difficulty in any part of their job, discuss it immediately. Failure to address the situation is likely to worsen it. Avoid taking action that may alleviate a problem in the short term but compound it in the future. By offering to complete the task under discussion yourself, for example, you will not equip the appraisee to cope if the same circumstances recur.

POINTS TO REMEMBER

- If an issue has a high impact on performance but is not urgent, it may be dealt with later.
- If an issue is urgent but has little impact on performance, it may also be left for another day.
- Issues that have a high impact on performance and are urgent must be dealt with immediately.

 59 Keep the tone relaxed but avoid time-wasting chat.

DOS AND DON'TS

☑ Do allow people to learn from their own mistakes.

☑ Do encourage people to think of ways of solving a problem.

☑ Do make your feedback and your agreements for the future absolutely clear.

☑ Do clarify the situation if an incorrect assumption has been made.

☒ Don't assume that you will have the best answer to a situation.

☒ Don't allow mistakes to cause people to fail in their objectives.

☒ Don't allow an appraisee to leave with an unrealistic view of their ability.

☒ Don't waste time discussing skills that the appraisee does not really need.

60 Under-promise during an appraisal and over-deliver afterwards, rather than over-promise and regret it.

CONSIDERING IMPLICATIONS

Bear in mind that what you say to an appraisee may have repercussions beyond the hour or so you spend with them. It is important to avoid agreeing to any action that may have an adverse effect on the team or on the organization itself. If, for example, you agree that an appraisee should attend an external training course to obtain qualifications that are not directly relevant to their job, this could create a precedent. The result of this may be that you find yourself being pressured by other members of the team to be given similar advantages.

MOVING FORWARD

At some point, both parties need to draw a line on the past and think of the future. This is particularly true if the past has been inherited and has left legacies that cannot be changed. When you come to the natural end of a discussion of the past, signal the time to move forward by talking about the action plan. Focus on future objectives and what you both think will work from now on. Talk about future milestones and deadlines that have to be achieved. Ask the appraisee to summarize the actions you have agreed, to check that you both have the same understanding of what has to be done.

FOCUSING ON THE FUTURE ▼

Encourage the team member to look to the future and motivate them by explaining how future action plans will benefit the appraisee, the team, and the organization.

Manager points out that time management course should put an end to having to work late

39

READING THE SIGNALS

Some people struggle to raise concerns in a straightforward manner. Understand the role that body language plays so that you can read an appraisee's body posture and facial expression to gauge whether they are holding back or responding positively.

61 Avoid reading too much into a single gesture – look for clusters of them.

62 If an appraisee looks tense, ensure that you look relaxed yourself.

IDENTIFYING ANXIETIES

You may need to coax an appraisee into speaking their mind, particularly if they are worried about what you will think, or do not know you very well. Begin with questions about easy and positive issues. Smile and maintain good eye contact. Watch for agitation and concern; this could imply that the conversation has turned towards issues they would rather hide. Listen to the content of replies and to the tone of voice used. Keep asking questions to get to the bottom of the matter, even if you are covering the same ground again.

WATCHING FACIAL EXPRESSION

When two people have a good rapport, they will look at one other throughout their conversation, turning away only to blink or think. The level of eye contact provides many clues to how your appraisee is feeling. If, for example, the appraisee avoids eye contact, there is probably a reason. Perhaps he or she does not wish to discuss the issue, is having difficulty in facing it, or is not telling the whole truth. Watch for changes in facial expression. If an appraisee looks away at a particular point, ask questions in that area to discover what is troubling them. Avoid taking notes when an appraisee is discussing an important point, since this will interrupt eye contact and prevent you from gauging their expression.

Head held straight but relaxed shows confidence

▲ **SHOWING OPENNESS**
By maintaining direct eye contact with you, this appraisee is signalling that a good rapport has been established.

CHECKING CONFIDENCE

Watch how an appraisee reacts to taking on each action as you proceed through the agenda. Look for any signals that they are not totally comfortable with what you are asking of them. It is important that the appraisee does not have reservations that will prevent them from achieving their objective. For example, if you are asking the appraisee to take on a new project or task, question them to assess their understanding of the task and their plan for carrying it out. You should be able to determine their level of confidence from their tone of voice and facial expressions as they answer. If the appraisee says "Yes", but in a hesitant fashion, this signals an undisclosed concern, or barrier, to achieving success. Use open questions to explore this area until you achieve the response of an unqualified "Yes", delivered in a firm tone of voice. Look out for phrases such as, "Yes, but …" and "Fairly happy …", since both indicate a lack of confidence. Continue the discussion until you receive unqualified agreement.

63 Watch an appraisee's eye movements – they can give a lot away.

CULTURAL DIFFERENCES

The Japanese tend to behave more formally than Europeans or Americans, which makes their body language more difficult to read. In the United States, body language is used to build rapport quickly, which may appear over-friendly and therefore be thought insincere by Europeans, who are more restrained.

Expression indicates undisclosed feelings

Tensing of the muscles around the eyes shows contemplation

Questioning expression indicates a lack of commitment

▲ **HAVING RESERVATIONS**
By looking downwards while thinking, this appraisee indicates that he may have some doubts, which you will need to explore.

▲ **FRAMING A RESPONSE**
This appraisee is looking straight ahead but not necessarily in focus, suggesting that he is visualizing how he should respond.

▲ **FEELING UNCOMFORTABLE**
By her expression, this appraisee is signalling that she lacks commitment to doing what has been asked of her.

ADOPTING THE RIGHT POSTURE

Always maintain an open posture, keeping your hands relaxed at your sides or in your lap. By being relaxed yourself, you will encourage the appraisee to relax, too. Make sure that the room is neither too hot nor too cold, but is at a comfortable temperature that encourages both of you to sit comfortably. Avoid crossing your arms, since this suggests either defensiveness or that you are putting up a barrier, and avoid leaning an elbow on the desk, which could be interpreted as an aggressive gesture. Remember that you are leading the discussion, so it is important to work at looking relaxed, even if you, too, are nervous at the outset.

CULTURAL DIFFERENCES

Body language conveys varying messages in different countries. In Latin cultures, for example, touch is used as a way of establishing and maintaining rapport. In more formal cultures such as in Japan, Scandinavia, and northern Europe, this would be considered an invasion of private space. A nod in Middle Eastern countries would signal disagreement rather than assent.

64 Remember that body language speaks more than words.

65 Be aware that if an appraisee leans back and crosses their hands, it signals reluctance.

NOTING AN APPRAISEE'S POSTURE

Look at the appraisee's posture. If he or she is perched on the edge of their seat, this suggests nervousness or anxiety. Relax them by using a friendly tone of voice, a smile, and plenty of open questions. If an appraisee places their elbows on the table, or clenches their fists, they could be feeling suspicious or even aggressive. Keep your own body language open, but neutral, and stress to the appraisee how the appraisal will benefit them.

DOS AND DON'TS

✔ Do observe what happens when you alter your body posture or expression.	✘ Don't interrupt or use a judgmental or condescending tone of voice
✔ Do check that an appraisee's body language matches their words.	✘ Don't look down at your notes for long periods, since this can reduce rapport.

MIRRORING BODY LANGUAGE

The study of Neuro-Linguistic Programming (NLP) provides further insights into the meaning of body language. One premise of NLP is that if two people are enjoying a good rapport, they will mirror one another's postures and use similar gestures. When one party leans forward slightly because they are interested in what is being said, the other party also tends to lean forward. When first-class rapport occurs, people may even mirror one another's breathing patterns. You can use NLP techniques to create empathy and ease tension by subtly mirroring an appraisee's posture. NLP practitioners also observe that people move their eyes according to what they are thinking. Thus you can gauge an individual's inner feelings by watching their eye movements.

66 Be aware of your own body posture at all times.

67 Encourage an appraisee with a friendly smile.

▼ **INFLUENCING POSTURE**
You can use mirroring techniques to alter the posture of an appraisee. By adopting a relaxed but alert posture yourself, you encourage the appraisee to mirror your positive body language.

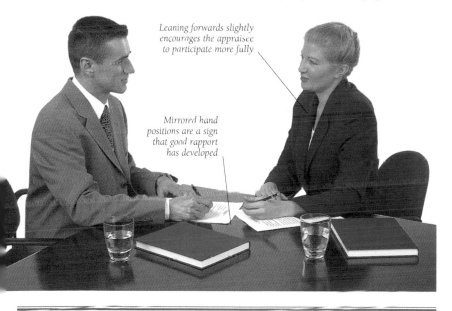

Leaning forwards slightly encourages the appraisee to participate more fully

Mirrored hand positions are a sign that good rapport has developed

ASSESSING COMMITMENT

People turn good intentions into achievement when they are committed to taking action. Check that appraisees take full ownership of their objectives before, during, and after the appraisal. If commitment is lacking, take steps to find out why.

 68 If you spot doubts, question until you gain an appraisee's commitment.

POINTS TO REMEMBER

● An appraisee who is not committed to taking action will nevertheless find ways to avoid saying a direct "No" to their appraiser's suggestions.

● The detection of a lack of commitment early on makes it easier to avoid problems later.

● An appraisee who feels that they have been pressurized into agreement is unlikely to be truly committed.

ANTICIPATING COMMITMENT

If you know an appraisee, you will be able to anticipate their level of commitment more easily. Consider whether they have agreed to undertake a task in the past but failed to deliver. Do they keep you up to date with progress regularly, or only when you intervene to ask for information? This knowledge will help you to decide how assertive you need to be to ensure that the appraisee is committed to carrying out action plans. If an appraisee is new to your team, you should make these judgments during the appraisal.

OBSERVING COMMITMENT

It is important to observe the degree of enthusiasm and commitment the appraisee shows towards agreed objectives and performance levels throughout the appraisal. There are a number of signs that an appraisee is becoming committed to the task. If, for example, they begin to elaborate on plans for achieving an objective, or start asking questions about implementation and who should be informed about the objective, these are positive signals of commitment. To test commitment, use a closed question aimed at prompting an unequivocal "Yes". If an appraisee is unwilling to commit, he or she will ask more questions, or voice doubts.

 69 Watch how keenly an appraisee accepts responsibility.

 70 Practical questions or suggestions indicate readiness to commit.

AGREEING REVIEW DATES

Encourage the appraisee to suggest an appropriate time to review progress in achieving milestones. In setting dates themselves, they take control of their own progress and will be more committed than if review dates are imposed. Before agreeing dates, take the appraisee's experience into account: more frequent reviews may be needed for inexperienced staff. Make clear any exceptions to the timetable, such as the need to be informed of any issues that could put a critical deadline or project at risk.

 71 Stress that you will not interfere – but that you expect to be kept advised.

 72 Be careful to avoid accepting a glib "Yes".

RECOGNIZING COMMITMENT ▼

Committed appraisees keep their manager well informed of progress, ask for help when needed, and discuss their tasks with colleagues. Uncommitted appraisees tend to avoid their manager and all discussion of the task at hand.

REVIEWING COMMITMENT

An appraisee who is committed to a task will prioritize it. If they find that they cannot achieve a date, they will try to negotiate extra time or suggest dropping less urgent actions in order to complete the task. If an appraisee has no intention of performing the task, you are unlikely to find out until after the deadline for completion. To review commitment, consider whether the appraisee approaches you with problems in good time. If you have to chase an appraisee, you must address why they have not taken ownership of their task.

POSITIVE COMMITMENT

- Shows enthusiasm
- Solves problems
- Reports on progress
- Displays initiative

POOR COMMITMENT

- Displays resignation
- Ignores problems
- Maintains silence
- Lacks initiative

HANDLING DIFFICULT SITUATIONS

An appraisal is almost certain to cause staff to worry, since their capabilities are under discussion and their future is at stake. Be prepared to deal with the unexpected, and learn how to handle difficult situations with authority and sensitivity.

73 Try to anticipate negative responses and plan how to deal with them.

HANDLING UNEXPECTED CHALLENGES

It is important to deal with challenges when they happen if you are to retain your credibility. If an appraisee challenges your authority, or your facts, try to deal with this at once. When you need time to think, use open questions to press the person to clarify their point. Should an appraisee reveal information of which you had no prior knowledge, or that sheds new light on a situation, check whether this affects the feedback you had planned.

Manager takes a long pause before calmly responding to challenge

Appraisee airs grievances and challenges manager's facts

Manager listens while appraisee speaks his mind

▲ DEALING WITH DIFFICULT PEOPLE

This illustration shows how, by remaining calm and framing her response with care, the appraiser was able to instigate a more productive discussion and agree actions to which the appraisee was fully committed.

RECOGNIZING YOUR LIMITATIONS

During the appraisal, your team member may reveal information that could affect their ability to do their job. You could discover, for example, that they have a serious illness which they had kept to themselves. Maintain a balance in your aims as manager. While it is important to motivate and build relationships with individuals, you must consider the success of your team and organization. Be sympathetic, but do not start altering the existing sickness policy at the appraisal.

74 Recognize when to seek guidance from colleagues or professionals.

75 Endeavour to remain calm and in control at all times.

Appraisee recovers and the discussion is concluded successfully

When progress is reviewed, appraisee is successfully carrying out action plan

Manager becomes irritated and interrupts appraisee

Appraisee reacts angrily, appraisal is stopped, and his performance begins to deteriorate

STOPPING THE APPRAISAL

In some circumstances, your only way forward may be to stop the appraisal. First, do all that you can to defuse a difficult situation. If an individual is upset, allow them to recover their composure and continue when you can. Be sympathetic if tears are genuine, but be wary of tears designed to deflect you from your feedback. Try to move on and get them to focus on the next agenda item, which, if you are following the praise, criticize, praise principle, should be more positive. If the appraisee has stopped listening, however, there is little point in continuing. Set a date to finish the appraisal as soon as possible.

DEALING WITH PERFORMANCE PROBLEMS

Tackling poor performance effectively is a challenge for all managers. Gain acknowledgment that a problem exists, then you can deal with it constructively by identifying causes and asking appraisees to come up with effective solutions.

76 Use good questioning techniques to explore solutions.

77 Avoid discussing problems that do not affect performance.

GAINING AGREEMENT

Before you can correct a problem, the appraisee must acknowledge that a problem exists. It is important that they realize the adverse impact of their actions on meeting their objectives, or they will not commit to solving the problem. Explain how their performance has affected that of their team or the organization. Ask questions to check that the team member has now accepted that there is a problem. Make sure that they fully understand where they have gone wrong and the impact of allowing the situation to continue.

IDENTIFYING CAUSES

Having gained agreement that a performance problem exists, explore the reasons and look for ways of resolving it. Ask the appraisee to analyze the cause; he or she may provide valuable insight into what has gone wrong. Some problems have multiple causes. If a person is falling behind with their work, for example, there may be a need for skills training. But are there other factors to consider? Watch out for excuses or blaming other departments – make sure that the appraisee takes the responsibility they should.

QUESTIONS TO ASK YOURSELF

Q Could problems with organizational processes be contributing to a shortfall in performance?

Q Is the machinery being used adequate for the job?

Q Is an insufficient budget holding the individual back?

Q Are the materials being used appropriate for the job?

ADDRESSING PERFORMANCE PROBLEMS

PROBLEM	WAYS TO ADDRESS IT
CAPABILITY The inability to perform the job as defined, perhaps as a result of a selection error or lack of experience.	● Provide support and training to enable the appraisee to tackle the job effectively. ● If training is not the answer, consider transferring the employee to a more suitable role.
TRAINING A lack of necessary skills or information that is preventing the employee from performing to standard.	● Identify gaps in knowledge, skills, or approach, and select appropriate development activities to help the appraisee meet required standards. ● Set objectives for continuous improvement.
MOTIVATION A decrease in effectiveness due to under-stimulation, or boredom, or stress resulting from too great a challenge.	● Identify development activities that will re-energize the appraisee in their role. ● Review tasks that have been delegated to the appraisee – are you over-stretching them?
DISTRACTION An inability to concentrate and be effective at work, perhaps due to a personal problem that is claiming an individual's attention.	● Be sympathetic. If necessary, agree time off work so that problems can be attended to. ● Recognize when to refer an appraisee to experts if performance fails to pick up.
ALIENATION A rejection of, and feeling of non-involvement in, the job and organization where there is a history of long-term frustration.	● Find out how the problem has arisen: is it the result of lack of challenge or neglect? ● Consider referral to a career counsellor to help the employee to resolve their issues

78 If an appraisee is reluctant to take action, stress the gains to be made.

FINDING SOLUTIONS

The best solutions are those that appraisees discover themselves. Ask the appraisee to come up with a plan to resolve or avoid the problem next time. Offer your own ideas only if necessary. Discuss the options before making a decision. If their solution is unrealistic, prompt them to discuss its advantages and disadvantages, or ask them to consider the risks associated with their proposal. By asking such questions, you can help the appraisee to choose a more workable plan of action. Finally, agree a short- and long-term action plan that will immediately bring performance into line, and then continuously improve it

DISCUSSING DEVELOPMENT

Training and development activities are aimed at helping appraisees to achieve their objectives and improve both short- and long-term performance. Choose activities and methods of learning to suit the appraisee, then agree on learning objectives.

79 Keep the long term in mind when planning development.

80 See that personal development plans are dynamic and kept up to date.

DEFINING DEVELOPMENT

Training and development activities are designed to continuously improve team members' skills and capabilities in their current roles, and to develop their future potential. They help staff to welcome and learn from change, work more effectively, and take on wider responsibilities. Activities are documented in personal development plans (PDPs), which map out current and future development goals. To agree activities positively, first talk to the appraisee about their strengths to show that you value their contribution. Then discuss areas where development is needed.

DOCUMENTING DEVELOPMENT ▼

Ask the appraisee to record their training needs and learning objectives on their personal development plan as you discuss them. Details of the activity should be recorded by the appraiser.

PERSONAL DEVELOPMENT PLAN

Name: NORMAN JACKSON

Development need	Activity	When	Learning objective	Results
To understand how to prioritize tasks, allocate sufficient time to each, and achieve tasks by deadline Tools and tips to help organize myself better would be very useful.	1 day time management workshop Value: £220 externally provided by external training provider	October	I will be able to plan my time more effectively and achieve what is important	● Learned tools and techniques to organize and plan my day more efficiently ● My performance has improved in that I can more effectively focus on important priorities

Appraisee should summarize training requirements *Appraiser describes activity with details of cost, and provider* *Appraisee should define what he hopes to gain from activity* *Appraisee should record outcome of training activity once completed*

CHOOSING A METHOD OF DEVELOPMENT

Training is often conducted on the job, with an appraisee being coached by their manager or a colleague, but other methods can be used to accelerate the learning process. Discuss the options with the appraisee to identify what is best for them. What is their preferred method of learning? Do they learn faster by doing a job themselves, or by having the job demonstrated to them? Do they enjoy reading, or would they gain more from computer-based learning? Decide on the method, when training should take place, and then plan the dates and make the necessary arrangements.

81 Ascertain what type of previous training has taught the appraisee most.

82 Encourage people to take up every opportunity for development.

SELECTING ACTIVITIES

The following are examples of possible development activities:

- Coaching and mentoring;
- Shadowing a colleague;
- Reading journals/books;
- Attending courses or workshops;
- Taking on delegated tasks;
- Attending project meetings;
- Being rotated in a role or transferred to a new job;
- Going on secondment;
- Attending conferences, briefings, or seminars;
- Studying for professional or work-related qualifications, such as first aid, health and safety, or business management.

WRITING LEARNING OBJECTIVES

Just as you agree clear business objectives with measures of success for appraisees, so you also need to establish what they should learn from undertaking training courses or other development activities. Defining learning objectives gives direction to training and allows you to monitor whether activities are meeting the needs of the team and its members. Consider what you want the learner to be able to do by the end of the activity, and how well you want them to able to do it. This gives you learning objectives with two constituents – a verb and a standard. For example, if you plan to send an appraisee to learn more about the service you offer to customers, a learning objective might be that at the end of training, the appraisee will be able to answer customer queries on three of your products. Even on formal training courses that already have general learning objectives, you should still tailor objectives to describe your appraisee's particular needs

DISCUSSING ASPIRATIONS AND POTENTIAL

Most people aspire to take on more senior roles and further their careers. Take the opportunity to discuss an appraisee's future aspirations and potential so that you can help them prepare for advancement in the future.

83 Talk about long-term prospects as well as short-term objectives.

PLANNING FOR THE FUTURE

Find out about an appraisee's aspirations for the future so that you can plan the support and development they need. Use open questions to explore how they envisage their current role changing over the next year. Then ask what the appraisee would like to be doing in, say, one to two years' time. Aim to identify development needs for both time frames. There are many ways of meeting development needs, such as special projects, site visits, or preparing to present to colleagues, that will enable an individual to gain more experience or skills.

Recognizing his potential, manager arranges training to help him further his career

Appraisee outlines his hopes of being promoted to a more senior role

▲ **BUILDING CAREERS**
This illustration shows how training an appraisee who is able to take on more responsibility benefits the organization, and how, when aspirations are not realized, the individual becomes frustrated and decides to leave.

ANTICIPATING CAREER MOVES

Be aware of your organization's policy on career development. Look at the career paths that other people in your organization, or team, have followed. This will give you a better idea of the career moves that might be possible and enable you to answer an appraisee's questions on the subject. If an appraisee is ambitious and has the potential, a move in one or two years may well involve transferring to another part of the organization. Even if you support it, do not agree to a potential move if you are not in a position to help it happen, or if it is not in line with company policy.

BENEFITING YOUR ORGANIZATION

It is important to keep the needs of your organization in mind throughout the appraisal. Complete any career development documentation, and make sure that the human resources department and senior managers know about people in your team who have potential. Avoid trying to keep people on the team for as long as possible because you have trained and developed them: remember that new recruits inject new ideas. Remember, too, that senior management prefers "net exporters" of team members to managers who hoard their own people. Aim to become known as a manager who develops and encourages people, since this will result in more people wanting to join your team.

Appraisee's aspirations are realized when he is promoted to lead a new project team

Appraisee receives no training, becomes demotivated, and decides to find a new job

DOS AND DON'TS

✔ Do look for ways of promoting people who are capable of doing more.

✔ Do plan how to replace people who are promoted off your team.

✘ Don't pass poor performers onto colleagues in other departments.

✘ Don't assume that your staff will be happy to remain in their current jobs.

Planning Action

In order for an appraisee to achieve objectives, it is vital that they know who is responsible for which actions and the deadlines for carrying them out. Agree and document a detailed action plan that sets out what needs to be done.

84 Ensure that someone is accountable for every action.

85 Always carry out your own commitments on time.

CREATING AN ACTION PLAN ▼

Draw up an action plan to provide a record of actions agreed. It may be no more than a simple note of chasing up information, or it may be a more detailed rundown of new responsibilities or projects.

Documenting Actions

Write down actions that arise from your discussion about objectives to ensure that you have a record of what has been agreed. This will avoid any misunderstandings or disagreements later. Use a prepared form, or ask the appraisee to use a notepad. Be careful to avoid dictating an action plan, since this will not encourage the appraisee to commit to it. As the appraiser, you may also be responsible for a few actions, primarily those concerned with resourcing training and development, or informing people in other areas of your organization that the appraisee has your authority to act.

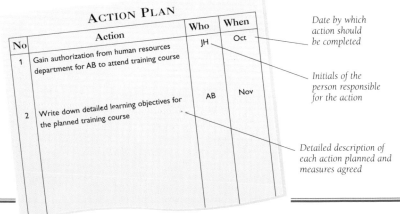

ACTION PLAN

No	Action	Who	When
1	Gain authorization from human resources department for AB to attend training course	JH	Oct
2	Write down detailed learning objectives for the planned training course	AB	Nov

Date by which action should be completed

Initials of the person responsible for the action

Detailed description of each action planned and measures agreed

PLANNING A PROJECT

A project is a series of activities designed to achieve a specific outcome to a set budget and timescale. Some of the objectives you agree may well constitute a project. If you assign a project to the appraisee during the appraisal, help them to use the discipline of project management to improve their performance. Make sure that you can measure success quantitatively and qualitatively. Finally, if you have any doubts about the appraisee's ability to complete the project successfully, address them. Decide how the appraisee can overcome the skills gap, or close it with training and development.

PLANNING DIARIES

To help the appraisee use their own initiative and take ownership of their objectives, it is important that you keep the actions that you agree to in an appraisee's action plan to a minimum. However, there may be issues that are beyond their control, such as ensuring that they are given the authority to manage a project or work towards an objective. Let the appraisee know what you need to do, so that you can both note the dates by which actions will be completed. After the appraisal, allocate the time and resources you need to enable you to support the appraisee's achievement of their objectives without doing their job for them.

ASSIGNING A NEW PROJECT

Establish the overall purpose of the project

Define the objectives of the project in detail

Outline constraints and find ways to tackle them

Ask the appraisee to list key milestones of the project

Agree on how achievement of milestones will be measured

Check that it is feasible for the appraisee to succeed in project

Appraiser notes dates for reviewing milestones and achieving objectives

AGREEING DATES ▶
Make sure that there are no discrepancies regarding what actions are expected to be done when, and by whom, by writing dates in both the appraiser's and appraisee's diaries.

SUMMARIZING THE APPRAISAL

Documenting a summary of the appraisal provides a vital record for both parties, and for the organization, of what has been agreed. Agree a detailed summary with the appraisee as a final check that they are committed to their action plan.

86 Listen carefully to what an appraisee says, and observe how they say it.

87 Avoid dictating to an appraisee – allow them to use their own words

INVOLVING THE APPRAISEE

Using their notes, or the form that they have filled in, let the appraisee summarize what has been agreed as a final check that they are committed to the action plan. If the appraisee finds it difficult to sum up the action plan in their own words, this indicates that they have not fully understood what needs to be done. Discuss those areas that are causing uncertainty to ensure that you both take away the same result from the appraisal.

CASE STUDY

Nigel's manager, Helen, had run out of time at the end of his appraisal. As a result, she had not asked Nigel to summarize the last action plan in his own words. The appraisal over, Helen was expecting Nigel to choose some stationery and order it from their usual supplier as part of a long-term contract. However, Nigel thought that he had been asked to choose the stationery and then approach several

suppliers for a quotation. The misunderstanding came to light the following day when Nigel explained to Helen that stationery could not be delivered on time. Helen asked why, and explained that it was not necessary to go out to tender. She then asked Nigel to state the actions he was going to take to meet the schedule. This avoided further misunderstanding and the stationery duly arrived just before it was needed.

◀ SECURING CONFIRMATION

By failing to ask Nigel to summarize an action in his own words, Helen paved the way for misunderstanding. Fortunately, the miscommunication came to light the next day, when she was able to rectify her oversight. This time, she asked Nigel to state exactly what his subsequent actions would be, clarifying the situation for them both, and ensuring the prompt delivery of the stationery.

CLEARING UP MISUNDERSTANDINGS

If an appraisee omits a vital point from their summary, or misinterprets an issue, respond immediately. The appraisee may have altered the content, or the tone of what was said, perhaps to avoid taking action. Do not allow a misunderstanding to continue, since it will be difficult to raise the issue again without damaging the credibility and trust you have built up. If you need clarification, ask the appraisee to repeat the point, or give your own summary and check that you are both on the same wavelength.

POINTS TO REMEMBER

- Misunderstandings are often caused by wishful listening – hearing only what you want to hear.
- It is best to get things right the first time.
- People should be allowed to express and summarize action plans in their own style.
- Misunderstandings that are allowed to continue can often result in a loss of trust.

88 You should both leave the appraisal with the same understanding.

SEEKING CONFIRMATION

Aim to end the appraisal with an agreement that is satisfactory to both of you. If there is no time to reach total agreement on important areas, arrange to discuss the issues again later. You have now completed the appraisal form, the personal development plan and/or the action plan. Produce copies of these for yourself, the appraisee, and, if required, for the human resources department

GETTING FEEDBACK

In order to develop your own skills, immediately after the appraisal ask the appraisee to give you feedback on how valuable the session has been for them. Find out how well the person thought you listened and whether the output, including action plans and personal development plans, has been worthwhile. Ask an open question such as, "How useful has this appraisal been?" Ask which parts were most useful and what could be improved upon. Giving honest feedback to an appraiser can be difficult, so observe their body language and listen to their tone of voice to ascertain whether they are being open, or keeping opinions to themselves. If you doubt their positivity, probe further until they voice any misgivings they were concealing. Ask for an additional evaluation later on (perhaps at a review session) with the question, "What results do you attribute to our last appraisal?"

FOLLOWING UP THE APPRAISAL

Following up after an appraisal is key to maintaining motivation and progress. Monitor activities and development, and evaluate the appraisee's and your own ability to benefit from the process.

MONITORING PROGRESS

To ensure that appraisals result in the long-term benefits they set out to achieve, progress must be closely monitored. Hold the correct types of review at the appropriate time, and understand how to conduct them effectively.

89 Hold a short review, even if an appraisee is making good progress.

90 Ensure that you understand how people are feeling.

91 Try to anticipate problem areas for the appraisee.

USING REVIEWS

Hold reviews to check that milestones are being achieved between appraisals, to identify strengths and recognize shortcomings, and to build confidence. Staying in touch with an appraisee's progress will motivate them to keep improving. Choose a type of review that is appropriate to the appraisee, according to their progress and competence level. Allow experienced staff to meet deadlines on their own as far as possible, but hold more frequent reviews for newcomers, those who have taken on challenging new responsibilities, or those whose objectives are particularly stretching.

DEFINING TYPES OF REVIEW

TYPE OF REVIEW	WHEN TO USE IT
QUICK UPDATE A spontaneous, short, and informal review with no agenda.	This is useful when people are handling a new task or role, or if something has just happened with implications for the staff member or project.
AD-HOC REVIEW A 10–15 minute review with the purpose of discussing a specific topic.	This is held if the appraisee or appraiser are concerned that an objective may be under threat and need to plan how to tackle the problem.
CHECKPOINT REVIEW A pre-planned meeting to monitor milestones as agreed with the appraisee.	This is used to check that progress is on target, objectives are being met, and all is progressing according to plan.
EVALUATION REVIEW A formal meeting held at the end of every project to assess its effectiveness.	This provides an opportunity to find out what has been learned, to check that objectives were met, and that they were appropriate.

CARRYING OUT REVIEWS

While it is important that you build in checkpoints to ensure that the expected progress is being made, avoid interfering to deal with minor mistakes. Instead, use reviews to ensure that both you and the appraisee understand the nature of progress to date. Ask open questions to encourage the appraisee to admit to problems, if they exist. Assess their level of confidence, and listen for unsolicited comments that might signal doubts that they can achieve what is required. If there is a problem that the individual is finding difficult to put right, offer your support, but do not press them to accept it if they turn it down. Your aim is to encourage them to take ownership of the activity, think problems through, and only then offer solutions. Avoid becoming too involved in detail, since this will result in too much of your time being taken up in review meetings and cause the appraisee to think that you do not trust them.

QUESTIONS TO ASK APPRAISEES

Q What has been achieved and what have we learned?

Q How well do you think that we have worked together?

Q Which factors have helped your progress and which have hindered it?

Q What further development needs have you identified?

Q How do you think what has happened so far might change the way in which we work together in the future?

Q Are you happy to take responsibility for carrying this improvement action forward?

Q Can you foresee any problems that could hinder your progress in the future?

IMPLEMENTING DEVELOPMENT PLANS

To help staff develop their skills and knowledge as agreed in the appraisal, consider which development activities are most suitable. Review development plans frequently, and help appraisees to monitor their progress as they implement them.

92 Promote the sharing of insights and experience among your team.

93 It is never too late for anyone to learn new skills.

PROMOTING LIFELONG LEARNING

Each team member has a unique set of skills, knowledge, and experience that shapes their attitudes and behaviour. Your team members may be aware of at least some of their strengths, but the feedback that you give during appraisals helps people to recognize all the skills, knowledge, and experience they have acquired. Realizing what they have learned, and continuing to learn new skills, increases confidence and promotes a willingness to use more initiative and take risks.

Discuss the development plan you agreed during the appraisal with each individual, so that they take ownership of it and become familiar with the continual process of learning and self-development.

DEVELOPING YOURSELF ▼
Learning should be a continuous process, no matter what your age. The more skills and experiences you acquire, the more confident and knowledgeable you become.

Manager seeks to improve her understanding of financial accounts

94 Encourage people to greet new challenges with enthusiasm.

IMPLEMENTING AND REVIEWING THE PLAN

Look for development activities that benefit the organization, the team, and the team member. If, for example, you know that the appraisee is keen on outdoor activities, such as climbing and sailing, it may be appropriate to send them on an outward-bound style course to learn how teams form and develop. Encourage team members to refer to their personal development plans and review the results of development activities frequently. Help them to develop transferable skills that they can apply to a wide range of situations. Agree changes to development plans that enable the appraisee to react to changing circumstances and customer demands.

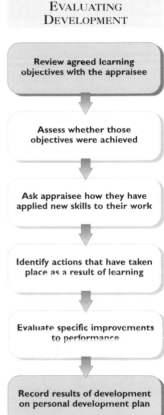

EVALUATING DEVELOPMENT

Review agreed learning objectives with the appraisee

Assess whether those objectives were achieved

Ask appraisee how they have applied new skills to their work

Identify actions that have taken place as a result of learning

Evaluate specific improvements to performance

Record results of development on personal development plan

▲ **BUILDING TEAM SKILLS**
By sending adventurous staff on courses in an environment that they will enjoy, you are helping them to learn team-building techniques that will be useful to their team and their organization. They will also improve their skills as a team member or leader in their favoured leisure pursuits.

EVALUATING TRAINING

Hold a de-brief session immediately after development activities to discuss how well learning objectives were met. De-brief after every type of event, including on-the-job coaching. If there is a gap between what was expected and what was achieved, discuss how to close the gap and update the development plan with that action.

ENCOURAGING TEAMWORK

The six-step appraisal system works just as well when used for teams as it does for individuals. Develop the skills and improve the performance of your team as a whole by holding regular team appraisals and integrating training needs.

95 Help people to realize how much they can learn from one another.

96 Praise team efforts to show that you value the fact that they pull together.

USING THE SIX-STEP PLAN

The six-step plan not only provides a framework for individual appraisals but is also useful in the team environment. Prepare the key issues for discussion, and call the team together for a combined appraisal on how well they are working together. Explain the purpose of the session and establish what team members' roles are. If there are issues that involve one or two people and not the whole group, postpone these to a separate meeting. As you work through the agenda, ensure that people write down their actions. Finally, ask everyone to summarize their own action plans to check their understanding and commitment.

USING TEAM APPRAISAL ▼

Focus team members on the objectives that they are seeking to achieve as a unit. Negotiate the agenda for the meeting, and be prepared to drop items that you have outlined for discussion in favour of better suggestions from team members.

Manager concentrates on discussing items that are of interest to the whole group

Team member prepares to summarize her own action plan at the end of the meeting

Team member notes actions for which he is responsible

97 Involve the whole team in planning its development for the future.

98 Get the most from a training budget by sharing resources.

ENCOURAGING TEAM FEEDBACK

Extend the use of the appraisal process to improving teamwork skills. Ensure that the entire team are clear about their objectives and how they are linked to other teams within the organization. As well as encouraging people to give and receive feedback during their own appraisal, help them to be open and constructive with each other. In the open environment encouraged by an effective appraisal, team members should be encouraged to share information and knowledge to build support and trust. Use team meetings to solve problems, build good working relationships, and review how the team is progressing against objectives.

INTEGRATING TRAINING

Group individuals with common training and development needs together so that training courses will be more economical. Keep a record for senior management of who have been attending courses, on which subjects, and the benefits. This will allow the management team to assess whether their investment in training and development is paying off in terms of business objectives. If senior managers are convinced by the business case for developing their staff, they will continue to invest. Future development plans are more likely to be approved if they build on past successes.

POINTS TO REMEMBER

- Just as consistency is needed within a single team, an organization requires consistency throughout all teams.
- Peers are often the best advisers to their colleagues.

ORGANIZING ▶ GROUP TRAINING
Plan to group people with similar training needs together. This is both cost-effective and strengthens staff relations, since team members can share learning experiences.

EVALUATING YOURSELF

F*or the appraisal system to work successfully, managers themselves must improve and develop skills alongside their staff. Evaluate your performance as an appraiser and ask your appraisees for feedback in order to become more effective.*

 99 Act as your own critic – but remember to be constructive.

 100 Take every opportunity to learn and practise new skills.

 101 Check that appraisals have win-win outcomes for all involved.

MONITORING PROGRESS

To ensure that appraisals have contributed to your team's continuous improvement, examine the results that each team member is achieving after the appraisals have taken place. Allow a period of, say, three months to see a noticeable improvement in performance. Check that the objectives set are consistent with the standards set for all individuals on your team. To help you do this, ask staff in similar jobs on other teams to give you a benchmark for performance. Ensure that the team's action plan has been implemented and that you have provided the promised support and resources. Finally, plan review sessions that are focused on performance improvement. Do the reviews demonstrate that clear progress is being made?

DEVELOPING YOUR APPRAISAL SKILLS

A valuable method of developing your appraisal skills is to practise role playing. Ask a colleague who understands the appraisee and his or her work situation to role-play how the appraisee might behave. If you have practised the answer to a difficult question, you will be able to answer it more authoritatively in the real meeting. Consider attending a training course on conducting appraisals. These generally tend to feature role playing quite heavily. If you do attend a training course, prepare notes on staff members you will have to appraise so that you will be able to use them as examples without breaching confidentiality.

EVALUATING THE LONG TERM

Review the entire appraisal process and all the appraisals you have conducted over the period of the past year. Reflect on what you have learned about yourself as an appraiser and how appraisal has helped you to achieve results. Only when you are slightly removed from the event will you be able to see patterns clearly and identify your development needs as an appraiser. Perhaps you need further training to be able to give feedback that is motivational, even when its content makes difficult listening for the appraisee. Perhaps you need to clarify roles or make objectives more measurable. Look at your timetable for appraisals and assess whether you allowed sufficient time for preparation, the appraisals themselves, and following up afterwards. Do you need to start earlier next time? How fair were the appraisals, and were they consistent for all individuals on your team? What have you learned about appraising over the year and, for that matter, about yourself?

▼ SEEKING FEEDBACK

To develop your skills as an appraiser, ask team members to give you honest feedback on your performance and the usefulness of their appraisals. Find out whether they were happy with the feedback they received, and if there are any aspects of the appraisal process that they feel could be improved.

Manager seeks feedback on the time allowed for staff to prepare for appraisals

ASSESSING YOUR APPRAISING SKILLS

E*valuate your ability to develop people through feedback and appraisal by answering the following questions as honestly as you can. If your answer is "Never", mark option 1; if it is "Always", mark option 4, and so on. Add your scores together, and refer to the analysis to see how you scored. Use the answers to identify the areas that need improving.*

OPTIONS
1 Never
2 Occasionally
3 Frequently
4 Always

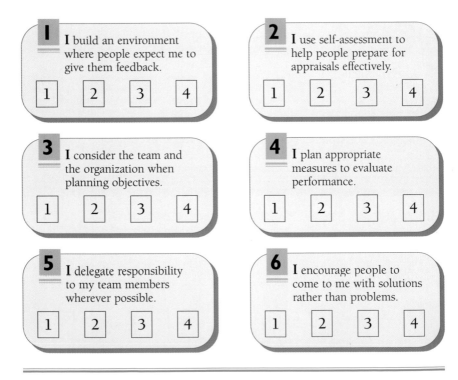

1 I build an environment where people expect me to give them feedback.

1 2 3 4

2 I use self-assessment to help people prepare for appraisals effectively.

1 2 3 4

3 I consider the team and the organization when planning objectives.

1 2 3 4

4 I plan appropriate measures to evaluate performance.

1 2 3 4

5 I delegate responsibility to my team members wherever possible.

1 2 3 4

6 I encourage people to come to me with solutions rather than problems.

1 2 3 4

7 I carefully consider which topics should be raised during an appraisal.

1   2   3   4

8 I prepare notes on the appraisee's past performance prior to their appraisal.

1   2   3   4

9 I identify ways of developing people when I prepare for their appraisal.

1   2   3   4

10 I am aware of what I can agree on my own authority in an appraisal.

1   2   3   4

11 I conduct appraisals in an atmosphere of trust and confidentiality.

1   2   3   4

12 I treat all staff equally and am fair and objective with every individual.

1   2   3   4

13 I plan how to deliver feedback constructively.

1   2   3   4

14 I explain the format that the interview will take at the start of the appraisal.

1   2   3   4

15 I agree the agenda at the beginning of the appraisal.

1   2   3   4

16 I listen far more than I speak during an appraisal.

1   2   3   4

17 I understand that what I say to an individual may have implications for others.

1 2 3 4

18 I am able to discover what is at the heart of people's anxieties.

1 2 3 4

19 I use my body language to help an appraisee to relax.

1 2 3 4

20 I ensure that appraisees are committed to carrying out their action plans.

1 2 3 4

21 I anticipate challenges that may occur in appraisals.

1 2 3 4

22 I ask appraisees for ways to solve problems before offering my own ideas.

1 2 3 4

23 I agree learning objectives before anyone attends a course.

1 2 3 4

24 I encourage people to consider wider opportunities throughout the organization.

1 2 3 4

25 I ensure that appraisees write their own action plans.

1 2 3 4

26 I ask an appraisee to give their summary of an appraisal first.

1 2 3 4

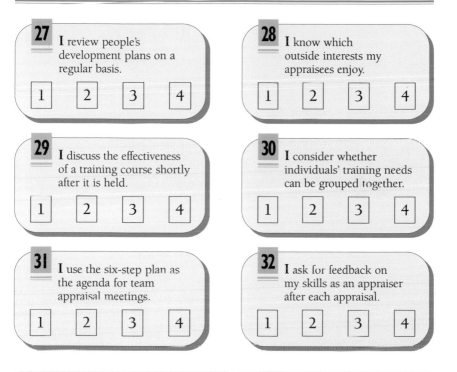

27 I review people's development plans on a regular basis.

1   2   3   4

28 I know which outside interests my appraisees enjoy.

1   2   3   4

29 I discuss the effectiveness of a training course shortly after it is held.

1   2   3   4

30 I consider whether individuals' training needs can be grouped together.

1   2   3   4

31 I use the six-step plan as the agenda for team appraisal meetings.

1   2   3   4

32 I ask for feedback on my skills as an appraiser after each appraisal.

1   2   3   4

ANALYSIS

Now that you have completed the self-assessment, add up your total score and check your performance. Whatever level of skill you have achieved in conducting appraisals, there is always room for improvement. Identify your weakest areas, then refer to the relevant sections of this book, where you will find practical advice and tips to help you refine your skills.

32–63: Your appraising skills are not yet sufficient to succeed in getting the best from people. Check that you are preparing as thoroughly as you should.

64–95: You are a reasonably proficient appraiser but you should identify areas for development and incorporate them into your personal development plan.

96–128: You are a good appraiser. Avoid complacency by seeking feedback from appraisees.

INDEX

ACKNOWLEDGMENTS

AUTHORS' ACKNOWLEDGMENTS

A book of this nature is very much a product of teamwork, and the authors were very impressed by the highly skilled people involved in its production. Adèle Heyward, Nigel Duffield, and Jamie Hanson at DK added greatly to the content of the book, while at Cooling Brown, Arthur Brown added his design skills and Mandy Lebentz proved again a motivating and meticulous editor. Our thanks to all of them.

PUBLISHER'S ACKNOWLEDGMENTS

Dorling Kindersley would like to thank the following for their help and participation in producing this book:

Photographer Steve Gorton.

Models Roger Andre, Phil Argent, Angela Cameron, Brent Clark, Jeanie Fraser, Sander de Groot, Emma Harris, Roger Mundy, Steve Newell, Kaz Takabatake, Suki Tan, Peter Taylor, Anastasia Vengeroua, Ann Winterborn, Roberta Woodhouse.

Make-up Janice Tee.

Picture research Cheryl Dubyk-Yates.
Picture library assistance Melanie Simmonds.

Make-up Janice Tee.

Picture research Anna Grapes.
Picture library assistance Melanie Simmonds.

Editorial Alison Bolus, Fiona Wild, Kate Bresler. **Indexer** Hilary Bird.

PICTURE CREDITS
Digital Vision: 23, **PhotoDisc:** 61, **The Stock Market:** Jose L. Palaez 4-5; Jeff Zaruba 63.

AUTHORS BIOGRAPHIES

Ken Langdon has a background in sales and marketing management in the computer industry. As an independent consultant he has advised many managers on the coaching, mentoring, and appraising of their staff. He has also lectured on strategic thinking and planning in the USA, Europe, and Australasia and has provided strategic guidance for many companies, including computer major Hewlett Packard.

Christina Osborne is a former director of personnel, an approved assessor and adviser in Investors in People, and has a wide experience in appraisals, coaching, and feedback. As chief executive of Business Solutions, a human resources consultancy, she has worked for ten years on integrating appraisals systems with the HR and business strategies of organizations in both the public and private sectors. She has sat on industrial tribunals, has lectured in business schools, and is a Fellow of the Institute of Personnel and Development and the Institute of Directors in the UK.